The Duke in

GW00734120

Susan Wear

The Duke in the Cupboard is based upon true events that are a matter of public record.

All rights in this play are strictly reserved and application for performance etc should be made before rehearsal to Southbank Communications, Kelvey House, Jarrow, Tyne and Wear NE32 5BH, 07949 765426.

If you wish to use the suggested music or film clips in a public performance, you will need to investigate the legal rights to do so.

ISBN: 978-1-7397 169-0-5

First published by KELVEY January 2022.

Printed & Bound by Martins the Printers Ltd of Berwick upon Tweed. Cover design by Graham Campbell.

Author's note

I'd like to thank Ray Spencer, and all the staff of The Customs House South Shields, Katy Weir, the original cast, Kempton Bunton's family, and my family - Jeff Brown, Alice Stokoe, Margaret and Alan Wear - for their help, support and inspiration.

I dedicate this print edition to all those fighting to protect the independence of the BBC with fair and sustainable funding that will allow free TV licences for those who can't afford them.

Susan Wear

January 2022

With love and all

best wishes

Susan Wear

Acknowledgements

The Duke in the Cupboard was first performed at The Customs House, South Shields 7 - 10 October, 2015, directed by Katy Weir.

The brilliant original cast and creative team were:

Kempton Bunton — Graham Overton
Dotty Bunton / Narrator — Zoe Lambert
John Bunton / thief #1 — Stephen Gregory
Bill Chester / thief #2 — Tom Machell
DI Homes / Judge / thief #3 — Scott Ellis
DS Stevens / QC / Duke — Adam Donaldson
TV arts correspondent — Jeff Brown

Movement Director — Kaine Husband
Set design — James Gardiner
Painting of the Duke of Wellington — Margaret Wear
PR and marketing — Leah Strug

4

Reviews

"*The Duke in the Cupboard* is Susan Wear's first play, and a remarkably assured one it is too." *British Theatre Guide*

"*The Duke in the Cupboard* is a warm, light-hearted play that highlights the frustrations of the individual battling against the system. Susan Wear should be very proud of her first play and Executive Director Ray Spencer needs commending for spotting the talent." *North East Theatre Guide*

"You can't help rooting for Bunton…. Along with plenty of good lines are neat touches of theatricality. I enjoyed the theft - cleverly done - and the appearances of the actual Duke of Wellington as his portrait starts to 'speak' to Bunton during his lonelier moments." *Chronicle Live*

Synopsis

In 1961 one of the world's most audacious art thefts shocked the nation. A portrait by Goya of the Duke of Wellington, idolised for defeating Napoleon at the Battle of Waterloo, had been snatched from under the noses of security guards at London's National Portrait Gallery. For the first half of the swinging sixties, detectives at New Scotland Yard were taunted by the mysterious perpetrator.

Whoever did it shinned up a 20ft wall, crept through two courtyards, climbed a ladder and squeezed through a toilet window, cleared a maze of electronic beams, lifted the painting, and went back the same way, unseen by anyone.

The first ransom note demanded £140,000 for charity. For four years the police were demented, calling in forensic scientists, criminal psychologists - even a medium. Little did they know they needed to look no further than Benwell, Newcastle.

What possessed a slightly antisocial, retired bus driver to leave his council house in Tyneside, hitch a ride to London - and take on the art establishment, the government, the police and even the legislature?

Based on an astonishing and heart-warming true story, this is the tale of a failed revolutionary, his long-suffering wife, an intrepid journalist, hapless detectives, surprises at the Old Bailey, and a mystery that is still not completely solved.

Characters

KEMPTON BUNTON
Aged 55, unemployed bus driver on disablement benefit living in a council flat in a deprived area of Newcastle in the North East of England - a Geordie. Weighing about 17 stones, he wears steel-rimmed glasses, a crumpled suit, shirts with detachable collars, a grey mac - often the buttons are fastened in the wrong place - and a trilby hat. Frustrated writer of poetry, plays and stories that are never been published. His manner of speech reflects the heavy wit and philosophy of the books he has read - Ruskin, Churchill, Shakespeare... Named by his father after Kempton Cannon, the jockey who won the 1904 Derby. Eccentric, antisocial with Victorian principles and set routines. Very clever at technology buying second hand radios, and even a printing press he fixed up in his living room.

DOTTY BUNTON
Aged 53, Kempton's long-suffering wife and mother of five. Hard to believe she was swept off her feet by Kempton but she admires strong principles. Still dresses like the smart office clerk she might have once have been although money is tight in their household. Modern outlook and loves the music of the day - a record player bought second hand and fixed by Kempton. Constantly chatting, spends most days with her daughter and granddaughter to escape the routine and monotony of living with Kempton. (Can double as the Narrator in the robbery scene)

JOHN BUNTON

Their 20-year-old son. Tall with fashionable haircut and side parting, Brylcreemed down. Left school at 15 with no exam passes but a cardboard folder of drawings and paintings as a reminder of failed potential. He drives a van delivering Wills Cigarettes all over the country. Loves the music of the day and dancing to the new groups appearing at the Oxford and the Dolce Vita. The apple of his Mam's eye, he reveres - and fears - his Dad. (Doubles as one of the painting thieves.)

BILL CHESTER

Rookie trainee on the local newspaper, trying to be confident and cocky - but a bit hapless. Too clever and gentle to be sent down the pit like his Dad He was supposed to be a librarian - but is determined to prove everyone wrong by becoming an investigative reporter in Fleet Street. Imitating older colleagues, he befriends people to get their stories but isn't good at it. Spends his days covering weddings, funerals. (Doubles as one of the thieves)

Det Insp MATT HOMES

Scotland Yard detective in charge of the case. Very experienced, proud, clever, but worn down by equally clever criminals. (Can double as the Duke, Jeremy Hutchinson QC and one of the thieves)

Det Const MIKE STEVEN

DI Homes's sidekick at Scotland Yard, young, eager to learn and irritatingly enthusiastic. (Can double as Judge Carl Aavold and one of the thieves)

THIEF #1	Unidentifiable, dressed in black head to toe.
THIEF #2	Unidentifiable, dressed in black head to toe.
THIEF #3	Unidentifiable, dressed in black head to toe.

THE DUKE OF WELLINGTON
General, former Prime Minister, hero of the British establishment
who trounced Napoleon at Waterloo. As painted by Goya.

JUDGE CARL AAVOLD
Senior Recorder at the Old Bailey.

JEREMY HUTCHINSON QC
Barrister for the defence.

NARRATOR
Narrates the robbery scene (can be played by Dotty)

RUSSELL WHITTAKER
TV Arts correspondent (recorded on film)

CHAIRMAN OF THE MAGISTRATES
(a member of the audience)

TIMING

1960 - 1969

SETTING

Newcastle upon Tyne in the early 1960s, a small council flat in the socially deprived area of Benwell. The play moves to Durham prison, the National Gallery, London, New Scotland Yard, London, a desk at the Daily Mirror, and back to the flat.

Loved the book,

Alastair - So here are these in return!

Also vividly remember telling my dad I loved him, after the funeral. If the father I one of my friends. So that bit made me cry!

We will enjoyed your company so much on our Grand Tour. Do let us know if ever your venture north again any time soon.

Will & Susan X

ISBN: 978-88-7393-029-7

9 788873 930297

Edizioni D'Arte I.F.I. Firenze

printed in Italy

ACT I

Scene 1

April 1960. *Opens in the kitchen/living room of a neat and tidy council flat in Benwell, Newcastle upon Tyne. An armchair in front of the TV, its back to audience; a pile of books on the floor by the chair; a polished wooden stereogram - record player - to stage right. The kitchen, with sink with gingham curtain, is visible to stage left. There's a pantry style cupboard door, and the door to the hallway both set to stage right. The external back door to stage left. A Formica top kitchen table and chairs to the front of the stage. A television set in the corner is tuned to ITV. The credits and music of "Emergency Ward 10" is playing. There is a lump of wood nailed across the television's tuner switch.*

KEMPTON is sitting in the chair.

KEMPTON: Dotty. Dotty! The door.

DOTTY (*enters*): I thought it was your hand you injured in that accident not your legs!

KEMPTON: I need to receive this visitor from here.

DOTTY (*sarcastic*): Oh, are you expecting somebody important? Is it the window cleaner this time or maybe the Lord High Admiral? Because I'm run off me feet answering the door to the milkman, the postman, Mrs Nebby Next-door and everybody else who has a mind to stick their nose in at your latest, stupid carry on.

KEMPTON: This "stupid carry on" will help millions of old people's lives - and I will go down in history.

DOTTY: Ha - you'll be going down all right if you're not careful.

She opens the door and brings in BILL. BILL enters hesitantly.

DOTTY (*putting on posh voice*): Come in! As you can see from the back of his baldy head, he's very busy watching Emergency Ward 10 on ITV, <u>not</u> BBC.

BILL: Hello Sir, I'm Bill Chester, from the Chronicle. Sorry to bother you, I was told you'd got a story for us?

BILL tries to get round the chair and tentatively offers his hand in greeting. Kempton stretches his arm backwards and they very awkwardly shake hands.

BILL: So, em, what's it all about Mr Bunton, or can I call you Ken?

He takes out his pen and notebook

KEMPTON *sighs, gets up and looks him up and down:* How long have you been a reporter?

BILL: Quite a while. I'm actually a trainee journalist, but they said I could do this one, since it was Benwell.

KEMPTON: I ask for the mechanic and I get the oily rag. No wonder the Chronicle never gets it right. (*Gestures at table*). Sit - you're about to get the scoop of your life.

BILL sits at the table, with notebook and fumbles in pockets for a pen. Turns to interview Kempton, but it's awkward because Kempton has sat down in the armchair again and has his back to him. Television continues to play.

BILL: Are you going to join me?

KEMPTON: Well I certainly cannot move from this position.

BILL: Why? Are you not well?

KEMPTON: No, I'm not ill. *(Stands up again and turns around)*. But you could say I am fighting a disease and looking for a cure against tyranny.

DOTTY, arms folded, rolls her eyes, grits her teeth and utters frustrated yowl...

DOTTY: I'm going to our Linda's to look after our grandchildren. And you Kempton you'd be better off coming with me.

DOTTY stomps off (exits)

BILL: Ah, OK, em Ken, what can I do you for?

KEMPTON: The name's Bunton, Kempton Bunton. Always has been since my father in his great wisdom named me after the famous jockey Kempton Cannon who won the Derby in 1904, the year before I was born. I can only guess he must have lost a few bob on that race and decided to take it out on me.

BILL (*writing in notebook*): So that's K, E, N, T, O, N...

KEMPTON (*jumps up)*: If you've ever heard of a jockey named after the posh end of Newcastle you'd be right, but no, here, I'll write it down for you.

BILL: Thanks. What's this scoop then, Ken, Kem...pton?

KEMPTON: The reason I cannot - couldn't - move from in front of the telly is that I am expecting Her

Majesty's Secret Service - AKA the Post Office
enquiry officers - to come and arrest me.

BILL: What have you done?

KEMPTON (*taking out his pipe*): Nothing.

BILL: Nothing? I have to say, it's not sounding like
much of a story? And I have to get to Wallsend
fire station before the watch changes. Blue Watch
is always quite good. Last night they had a cat
stuck in a drainpipe over Woolworth's in
Wallsend High Street. Great story - you wouldn't
believe the cat was called Rover. Who calls a cat
Rover?

KEMPTON: Right well here's some proper front page
material. On the 29th of April I was fined £2 for
using a television set without a licence by the
Justices of the Peace sitting on the bench at
Newcastle Magistrates' Court. As you can see my
set is fixed so that I get ITV independent
television only.

BILL: So? Still not much of a story... sorry, I mean, I
can't cover a court case if I wasn't there - it's in
me 'Essential Law for Journalists', Mr Bunton.

KEMPTON: You are staring at the elusive exclusive you are
desperately seeking, Mr Chester.

BILL (*looks around*): Am I? So are you just sitting there, or is
there anything else? Is the cat stuck somewhere?

KEMPTON (*sighs and moves to the table*): You could help make
this very big news and turn your career from local
hack to international fighter for social justice -
haven't you heard of the great Harold Evans?

14

BILL: No, did he play for Newcastle?

KEMPTON: No man! Anyway, I'm going to launch me campaign now. I told the magistrates: if you fine me, I won't pay. I'll go to jail. I'm making a stand on behalf of all the old folk who can't afford £4 for a television licence.

BILL: We all have to pay it though. Me Mam paid for me Nan's for Christmas last year. Mind I think she liked the Badedas Bath and the Black Magic I got her better.

KEMPTON (*interrupts him. He's tapping the pipe, chewing it, not smoking*): So that was seven days ago. Now I'm waiting to be arrested and taken to prison. And in the meantime, I'm going to keep watching the telly. The picture is good. *(He adjusts the knob on the front of the TV).* And offered free from the ITV.

BILL: Why you though?

KEMPTON: Ah, finally a good question. I met an old chap on Northumberland Street at the bus stop. His son had given him a second-hand television set. But he couldn't afford the licence - and he was terrified, petrified, to use it in case he was summoned.

It just stuck with me - and once I realised the plight of these old people I knew I had to fight. I fixed the set with a nice bit of wood nailed over the BBC switch - see! And you know what lad? Your story will help turn around this travesty of justice. And what do you think your Nan will make of that?

15

BILL *(open mouthed and backing out)*: It's not me Nan I'm
worried about. It's me news editor. If I don't get
a story out of this I think I'll be put back on the
tea trolley.

Lights down - sound of typewriter clacking / returning

Transition: Bill writing article.

Music: *The Who - Won't Get Fooled Again*

Blackout

ACT I

Scene 2

Two weeks later.

BILL, JOHN and KEMPTON are back in the Bunton's flat. BILL is sitting at the table. There are a handful of papers / newspaper cuttings and assorted letters on the table.

BILL (*shuffling through the letters and cuttings*): Is that it? Four? Only four people saw my story and bothered to write in support?

JOHN: Three, actually.

BILL: Three! What about the fourth?

KEMPTON (*Gets up and switches off the TV*)

JOHN: Someone called "Anonymous" wrote in...

KEMPTON: ...saying I was a common criminal who deserved to go to jail with the rest of the criminal fraternity of Benwell... and I could stick my licence, shall we say, where the sun doesn't shine. I think he was from Jesmond.

BILL (*picks up one of the letters*): I don't believe it. This one's from my Nan.

KEMPTON: Yes, she was very nice, very proud of you. She says would I mind not involving you and getting you into trouble.

BILL: Mr Bunton?

KEMPTON: Yes?

BILL (*moves towards him with disingenuous concern, only half serious, pen and notebook ready):* How does this make you feel?

KEMPTON (*rolls eyes*): Just write this down. I am amazed at the apathy of people when you remember so many of these old 'uns fought in two world wars to keep Britain free. We should keep viewing free for them.

BILL: So what next for the campaign then?

KEMPTON (*stands up, thumbs in braces, looks up as if making a speech but as usual hesitates over the grammar*):

I would suggest that red tape be cut, precedent forgotten and a quick act passed through the House of Commons allowing aged folk to take for nothing that which is already offered free. And I will write to Mr Ernest Popplewell, the MP, about the matter.

(Turns back to Bill.)

BILL: Your father was a betting man. What are your chances of winning?

KEMPTON (*affronted*): Be assured I've never gambled in my life. But what are my chances? God knows it's not as if I'm asking for much - it's not as if I think these pensioners are going to get free bus passes or cheap seats at the pictures!

But I think the odds would be better if a few more people knew what I'm doing.

JOHN *is making tea.*

BILL: Shall I put 100 to one then?   So, would you say
                you were a disappointed man?

KEMPTON: No man, I've just said - put this down - the fight
                goes on regardless. People are apathetic - look
                how many followers Jesus had when he started.
                Twelve - and one of those denied him and the
                other turned him in! Look at... Mahatma.

BILL: Who?

KEMPTON: Mahatma - Gandi - he started with nothing but a
                bit of cloth, like, and *(picks up the SAXA salt
                drum)* a grain of salt!

BILL: What's that got to do with free telly licences...

KEMPTON: He started a massive protest - against the salt tax.

BILL: The what?

KEMPTON: It was imposed on them by the British. He had a
                march - you know, like the Jarrow March? - for
                240 miles. And every town he went to he made a
                grain of salt in the sea and he refused to pay tax
                on it. And he went to prison for nearly a year.
                But in the end 80,000 more Indians went to prison
                for taking a stand against the British trying to tax
                them for something that is free. Just like the TV
                licence.

BILL: Does that mean you need 80,000 Indians?
                There's not many of them in Newcastle Mr
                Bunton.

KEMPTON: No - I just need me own army to fight against the
                Government. Salt - TV licence - it's just the
                same. Another bloody monopoly on free stuff

                              19

that this Government thinks it can get away with.

BILL: Monopoly? So maybe you could do a march next then? You might be able to make salt at South Shields beach?

JOHN splutters over tea.

KEMPTON: You know there's no monopoly on standards of the Great British press.

BILL: I see you take the Mirror as well as the Chronicle - that's where I'm going - Fleet Street.

JOHN: God help them. What do you want to be down among them southerners for?

KEMPTON: Anyway Mrs Bunton will be home in time for Candid Camera. And hopefully the Old Bill will be here soon....

Blackout

ACT I

Scene 3

A few months later, 1960. The Bunton's living room

DOTTY with her head down, curlers in, dressing gown sitting at kitchen table. Music: Cathy's Clown by the Everly Brothers is playing on the record player. JOHN is reading The Chronicle.

DOTTY: We'll have to cancel that now your Dad's gone.

JOHN: He's not dead Mam. He'll be back - he just got 13 days.

DOTTY: Oh the shame of it. How did it get to this? Woken up in the middle of the night in our beds - like common criminals.

JOHN: It's what he really believes in Mam. We should be helping him not ashamed of him.

DOTTY *(gets up and turns the record off)*: At least that daft lad reporter hasn't been sniffing around. I don't want you telling anybody mind. I've gone through enough without having to face her next-door strutting round like the Queen of Benwell telling everybody we can't afford to pay four quid for a TV licence. It'll kill your Nan if she finds out about this. I don't know how I'll show me face at the Co-op with them knowing all of our business.

JOHN has opened the paper. With a sharp intake of breath tries to hide it behind him.

DOTTY: What now? Give me that!

JOHN: Mam, Mam, I think you better sit down.

21

DOTTY: Come on what is it?

JOHN: Calm down Mam, it isn't a big story. (*reverently*) But it's what Dad would have wanted.

DOTTY: Ah haway John, he's not dead! (*She sees the headline and tries to grab the newspaper*) Oh bloody hell - are they kidding? What does that say?

JOHN: Mam! Stop it man!

She chases him round the table and stops, shouting:

DOTTY: John!

JOHN hands her the newspaper.

DOTTY *hands it back.* I can't read it without my glasses. Tell me what it says.

JOHN: It says: "The knock expected by Mr Kempton Bunton - Newcastle's television rebel" - there you are Mam, he's "Newcastle's rebel", not just Benwell - "came late last night".

DOTTY: Who's told them that?

JOHN *(keeps reading):* Soon after 11 pm two plain clothes policemen called at Mr Bunton's home in Yewcroft Avenue to arrest him. "He was told by the city magistrates in May that if he did not change his mind he would go to prison for 13 days. *(He hesitates, drops his voice.)*

Then it says, "My father had been waiting for some time for the police to come" - said 19-year-old John Bunton last night. I'm 20!

DOTTY: What! Did you tell that reporter - I can't believe you did that our John.

JOHN: I'm sorry, sorry. He just asked us to see me Dad and I told him he wasn't here. He sort of put two and two together like.

DOTTY: You idiot.

JOHN: What am I supposed to do? He's me Dad. We should be with him all the way.

DOTTY: I know, I know - but I just didn't bargain for this John. He's just not the man I...

JOHN: He is a bit... different.

DOTTY: He's four stones heavier for a start!

JOHN: But being different - that's what I like about him Mam. He really believes in stuff and he's like a rebel, a freedom fighter - just like Che Geuvara - or Al Capone.

DOTTY: I know you're loyal to your Dad John but he's no hero...

JOHN: He's got his principles.

DOTTY: Principles! What use are they - he's never had a job more than a few months - every time he gets one he loses it because he argues over some principle with his boss!

JOHN: He's got dreams.

DOTTY: Dreams! More like nightmares. He wants to be the next Winston Churchill and he can't even fasten his own coat!

23

She waves the newspaper - picture shows the wrong buttons are
fastened on KEMPTON'S old mac. And picks up the scissors.
She cuts the newspaper into squares. Pokes a hole through one
corner and ties them together on a loop with the string.

> There you are - we won't need to go to the Co-op
> now. Go and put it in the lavatory. And John,
> when he gets back, he won't do it again will he?

Blackout

ACT I

Scene 4

The scene setting is indicated as outside, at the top of the Bigg Market, Newcastle, near the offices of the Newcastle Chronicle. KEMPTON is standing on a wooden crate

KEMPTON: Ladies and Gentlemen! I have been fined £10 by the Newcastle Magistrates for watching television without a licence for the second time. I refuse to pay.

BILL: Are you giving yourself up now Mr Bunton? It's gathering a bit of interest now - MPs asking questions in Parliament.

KEMPTON: I expect to be in prison for the second time soon.

BILL: Hasn't somebody offered to pay the fine for you?

KEMPTON: How stupid would that be? If it's paid there will be no publicity.

BILL: But it'll be different in Durham jail.

KEMPTON: Don't worry about me. They've even got television in Durham jail now.

BILL: Only for the lifers... ...You better get going. Seems appropriate doesn't it.

KEMPTON: What?

BILL: The police station. Its name.

KEMPTON: What do you mean?

25

BILL: Its name - Arthur's Hill. It's like you really are going into battle.

KEMPTON: You're right - and seeking my own holy grail. There's one thing you can write though Bill. As soon as I get out again, I'll be keeping up the campaign.

BILL: You're mad you know.

KEMPTON: But if nothing has happened by next January, I will just give up watching television in disgust.

BILL: Let us know how it goes - don't talk to any other papers mind.

KEMPTON: Don't you worry.

Blackout

ACT I

Scene 5

*A cell in Durham Prison. The kitchen table becomes a sparse
bunk bed. Kempton is sitting on the bottom bunk, writing.*

Music: *Matt Monroe - Portrait of My Love*

*Spotlight on BILL stage right. He is reading KEMPTON'S letter
out loud:*

BILL: For attention of Messr. Bill Chester. Cell D2-69,
                   Durham Jail, Thursday.

                   My home is a cell more than a century old. Yes,
                   Kempton Bunton, late of 12, Yewcroft Avenue,
                   Newcastle, is now Prisoner No. 6379 of Durham
                   Prison. They brought me here in a chauffeur-
                   driven vehicle, welcomed me with many
                   questions at reception and gave me a luxurious
                   bath.

                   I was handed my sole possession - my pipe. I
                   asked for tobacco and matches - but no dice.
                   Next I visited the tailor and received my new
                   outfit. Then I was shown to my room.

                   All was silent except for the jingling of keys as
                   each door we went through was unlocked and
                   locked again behind me. As I stood waiting for a
                   cell I looked up at the cells piled many storeys
                   high. Long rows of them. There must have been

some 900 men all within easy distance of me and yet there was only this silence. It was eerie.

The door was banged and the keys jangled for the last time. My cell is newly decorated - with the sour odour of whitewash. I was happy to make my own bed with the sparse blankets provided.

But the only real fault I can find with the place is the three-inch-thick wooden door. It somewhat restricts my freedom.

Blackout

ACT I

Scene 6

JOHN and DOTTY are back in the Bunton's kitchen.

Music: Three Steps to Heaven by Eddie Cochran. They are dancing around a bit. The phone rings. JOHN picks it up.

JOHN *(speaking into phone):* Aye thanks Bill. He'll be really pleased.

DOTTY *(comes in taking headscarf of)*: Who's that on the phone?

JOHN: Nobody. Bill.

DOTTY: Oh get him off.

JOHN: Shh Mam. Yes, it looked good. It's just me Mam. Are you needing another angle for your story Bill, because I was thinking...?

DOTTY: You just keep that zipped John boy.

JOHN: Shurrup! Yes, no not you Bill. I was only thinking it would be good to talk about me Dad's plays... Aye, aye, we hope the Prime Minister writes back. I'll let you know. Thanks again. Turrah.

DOTTY: Well? What now?

JOHN: Good news Mam. He got his poem from a cell published!

DOTTY: A poem? Oh great. Now he thinks he's Shakespeare. I thought Mahatma Gandi was bad

29

enough. Please tell me John this is nearly over?

JOHN: Cup of tea then? He's pretty incredible to go through all this isn't he.

DOTTY: Yeah, incredibly stupid. You know what I really think? When he comes home he'll just get rid of his darned television set because though he won't admit it, I think even he's had enough.

JOHN: Bill said Dad's tried to write to me, but they won't let him.

DOTTY: He shouldn't involve you John.

JOHN: He said Dad's asked to see the Governor and complain about Freedom of the Press.

DOTTY: Too much to expect he'd just sit out his time quietly.

JOHN: He'll be home soon enough. November 4th by my reckoning. Should we tie a yellow ribbon on the door?

DOTTY flays her arms as if to slap him.

KEMPTON enters carrying a brown paper parcel of prison belongings, looking dishevelled. Tense moment where you think he might go up to DOTTY. He tips his trilby hat, nods at her and goes to sit in the armchair.

JOHN: Dad!

DOTTY (*jumps up shocked, pats her curlers, takes off apron, smooths dress*): You're back!

KEMPTON: I got a few days off for good behaviour - or

30

maybe to keep me quiet about the infringement of human rights and press freedoms. Cup of tea would be fine Mrs B.

DOTTY (*sarcastic*): Sit down won't you. Let me get your tea and your slippers and let's just get back to normal like nothing ever happened.

JOHN: What was it like Dad?

KEMPTON: It was an experience.

JOHN: Was it bad?

KEMPTON: The worst thing was that they refused to let me write to my own son. Not that it was the Governor's fault, just the regulations he has to carry out.

JOHN: Why?

KEMPTON: No idea. "Prison officials refused to comment".

DOTTY: What was in the letter?

KEMPTON: Nothing much - punishment, religion and education.

DOTTY: Nothing much!

KEMPTON: I just happened to mention that there were three of us in one cell and that there was plenty of space, as long as one of us sat on the ceiling.

DOTTY: Nothing to take offence at there then....

KEMPTON: And that the wages for sewing mailbags were actually two and tuppence and not enough.

31

DOTTY: Can't imagine why they wouldn't let you send that to the papers.

KEMPTON: It's the point of justice - being done and being seen to be done - and...

DOTTY: And what else?

KEMPTON: The chapel services. What was the point? Half the congregation slept right through them. They shouldn't be compulsory.

DOTTY: Aah, also a little bit controversial then. Anything else?

KEMPTON: The education.

DOTTY: Really?

KEMPTON: I learned two good lessons from the two gents I shared the cell with. One, how to knock a car without getting nicked - and two, how to carve the coppers up in three easy lessons.

DOTTY: No wonder they wouldn't let you write that Kempton!

JOHN: Honestly? How do you steal a car?

KEMPTON: Seems garage showrooms leave the car keys on the floor of the car. It's called slippin'.

JOHN: Slippin?

KEMPTON: Yes. You slip in, start the engine and drive it away. But you have to avoid the bait car.

DOTTY: The bait car? I'm guessing that's not about the sandwiches?

KEMPTON: No, man, it's when the police have set it up to try catch the criminal. There's usually a big white easy-to-spot van nearby.

DOTTY: And why did you want to tell everyone that?

KEMPTON: I didn't. The point I was making was that being in prison is for punishment but it does not help anyone reform and learn how to live a good life. People come out worse and educated only for a life of crime.

JOHN: That's brilliant Dad.

DOTTY: Kempton, why does it always have to be you? Is it all over now?

KEMPTON (*rising for a* speech): At 13 years of age I served on board the SS Monica and helped fight the U-boat menace in the North Sea.

DOTTY: Here we go - it wasn't the same when you refused to join up the second time was it?

KENTON: As a free Englishman I reserved the right to follow my conscience. And now I am in another war - and I'll keep it going for the sake of a million, aged, poverty-stricken people.

DOTTY: Oh God when will this stop?

KEMPTON: January 1st 1961. I realise it is probably a lost cause now but if there isn't another case brought against me before January I will go to the court penitent - and give up.

DOTTY: I'm off to the Bingo.

33

She exits.

Blackout

ACT I

Scene 7

New Year's Eve 1961.

Remnants of Christmas decorations in the kitchen.

Music: What do you want to make those eyes at me for by Emile Ford and the Checkmates.

DOTTY *(flitting around the kitchen)*: Tonight's the night!

KEMPTON: If you mean it's the last night of the year that's very interesting.

DOTTY: The night I get my television back.

KEMPTON: Don't be stupid - there's no television going on in this house.

JOHN: Dad, Mam...

DOTTY: It's ok. *(pause)*. I've already done it. I've paid it. Our Mary lent me the money. So there.

KEMPTON: You've done what? Have you gone off your head? After everything I've done?

JOHN: It's ok Dad. I've sorted it.

DOTTY: Kempton, calm down. You've done your bit. Why should it be down to you to fight for other people? Let's face it all they want is Dick Barton and the Light Service.

KEMPTON: Woman do not make light of this.

DOTTY: Make light? What! I've suffered Kempton - it's

not nice going to court and watching you be sent down - and not just once. It's not very nice prison visiting - twice. It's embarrassing facing the neighbours. It's horrible having reporters knocking on the door. And I really don't know how to explain it all to our own kids either. Apart from John who for some reason still thinks you're the bee's bloody knees...

KEMPTON: Are you finished?

JOHN: Dad!

DOTTY: No I'm not finished. When will you get it that nobody cares? The union's not helping, the MPs aren't interested - and I guess the councillors are too busy doing whatever Newcastle councillors do.

KEMPTON: What the heck has any of that got to do with this? I've met people in prison who have been banged up for a lot less than the goings on at that civic centre...

DOTTY: You're obsessed man. People think you're bonkers. You know I'll always stick with you Kempton Bunton. But - *(choking back tears)*. I missed - Princess Margaret's - wedding. *(She kneels, sobbing beside the armchair where KEMPTON has sunk)*

It was the dress Kempton. I only saw it in the bloomin' Chronicle. And I only got that because it was wrapping up fish and chips *(sob)* so there was a greasy mark on - Anthony Armstrong Jones's head. And you know, it was a... a... a Norman Hartnell!!!

KEMPTON (*stands up from the armchair and straightens his tie*): You can take the licence back. I will pay your sister back the £4. You will not be watching the BBC in this house tonight, tomorrow or any time.

DOTTY: You can't stop me. I am going to put it on right now. You can't give me one good reason why not. Or that really is it for you and me Kempton.

DOTTY moves to the TV set and grapples for the cable.

JOHN: You can't Mam.

DOTTY: Why not?

JOHN: I cut the plug off.

KEMPTON exits. DOTTY holds the plug-less cable and gestures angrily, exasperated, up at the ceiling.

DOTTY: So help me if I miss Coronation Street again I'll swing for him. If the bugger doesn't get himself hanged first.

She gestures - breathes - puts the record player on very low, plays

Only the Lonely, by Roy Orbison

JOHN: Mam you never swear.

DOTTY: Eeh John ... How did it get to this??

JOHN: Mam...

DOTTY: I could have had any of them teddy boys - they're all smoothy salesmen working in Harker's furniture department now, no doubt earning a fortune, probably buying their wives a mink coat

37

from Marcus the Farrier and shoes from Amos Atkinson.

But oh no, I choose a man who looks like he's been dragged through a hedge backwards, fixes his glasses with electrician's tape and with a name that sounds like some sort of - friend of Billy Bunter. And then he decides to take on the world and ends up in court and in prison.

I should have known - he was late for his own wedding because he was selling the Socialist Worker. I can't believe I'm saying it but I think me Mam was right.

JOHN: Mam! (*exits*)

She puts music on the record player - You don't have to say you love me / Dusty Springfield

KEMPTON *returns, wearing his mac, hair slicked back*: Pub? You coming Mrs B?

DOTTY (*sarcastic and sad*): I can't stay in and watch the telly, can I?

KEMPTON: Come on Mrs B. Anyway, I've reconsidered.

DOTTY: Really?

KEMPTON: I am sorry - I said I'd fight for a year and that year is up. I'm just disappointed, man. But I'll stick to my word. I'll give it up tomorrow. I'll look for a job.

DOTTY: What sort of job?

KEMPTON (*thinks*): I am a former wrestler.

DOTTY: A wrestler?! You mean that time you joined Silver Lonnen boys' boxing club for the week?

KEMPTON: You don't know everything about me. I am man of mystery. And I might make a useful security guard in these days of spivery.

He lunges at her in mock wrestling stance.

DOTTY: And I might be a bunny girl.

KEMPTON: I think I will start a fund instead. I'll call it the TV for the Aged Fund.

DOTTY: Snappy. But you've got no money.

KEMPTON: I've got other means.

DOTTY: Have you really? What?

KEMPTON: This morning I posted my play to the head man at the BBC and another copy to the head of ITV and I've asked them to bid against each other for the rights. Whoever wins can send a big cheque made out to TV for the Aged Fund care of the Lord Mayor of Newcastle or another suitable luminary.

DOTTY: You really think that's going to work, don't you?

KEMPTON: Yes. I am a writer. And now I've got a profile as well. It won't be long before I break through.

DOTTY: You'll be breaking down never mind breaking through. You said you'd given up!

KEMPTON: I have, I have, but you know I am a man of principle and I still have to do something.

DOTTY: I can't win, can I? Get your principles over here

Kempton Bunton.

They dance slowly to the music.

DOTTY (*pulling away):*   Where we going?

KEMPTON: The Crown?

DOTTY: I wasn't expecting La Dolce Vita.

She exits, KEMPTON lifts the record player arm on the way out. The music fades.

Blackout

ACT I

Scene 8

August 1961.

In the Bunton's living room. KEMPTON is watching television.

RUSSELL (*speaking from the television, reporting from location outside National Portrait Gallery on TV screen):* ... painting of the Duke of Wellington has been saved for the nation after the Government paid £140,000 to make sure it remains in the UK.

KEMPTON *(speaking over the television):* I don't believe it. What a load of rubbish. How the heck can they justify that?

RUSSELL: The portrait by Francisco Goya, was due to be taken to America by the millionaire oil baron and art collector, Mr Charles Wrightsman who intended to make a present of it for his wife, the New York socialite, Jane.

KEMPTON: That would have paid for thousands of television licences. A hundred and forty thousand pounds for a dollop of paint on a bit of canvas.

RUSSELL: Known as the Iron Duke, the Duke of Wellington, was the heroic commander who trounced Napoleon at Waterloo, saving Britain and Europe. The painting will be back in its rightful place on show to the public at the National Portrait Gallery from August 3rd.

KEMPTON *(gets up and switches off television):* The world's gone mad.

41

DOTTY: Calm down. It's just a painting.

KEMPTON: It's just the injustice of it. Can they not see how important having a television is for so many old people?

JOHN: What's happening Dad?

KEMPTON: The Government is taxing old people so they can't have a little bit of entertainment in their own home, so that rich people can go and stare at an old bourgeoisie warmonger's face whenever they like in a posh gallery in London. Who the heck does this Wellington think he is anyway?

JOHN: I think he invented wellies.

DOTTY (*joining the joke*): Aye he had a canny beef recipe as well. Eeh we shouldn't - the Duke of Wellington's a national treasure!

KEMPTON: Can you imagine John, a man in a desert in Texas, who makes his fortune digging oil out of the ground, which belongs to all of us by the way, or at least the indigenous Indian American peoples... has so much money he can go and buy just about anything he fancies.

And then we're all really grateful that he gives the thing back to allow the Great British public to buy back that which belonged to them in the first place - from themselves for themselves.

DOTTY: I know, and he was going to give it to his wife. I bet she's really annoyed.

Both exit. **Blackout**

42

ACT I

Scene 9

NARRATOR takes place at microphone, stage left. A painting is standing on an easel. THIEF #1, THIEF #2, and THIEF #3 perform choreographed movements to indicate Milk Tray advert / Pink Panther stealth style scene. The thieves all in black are ambiguous - they could be fit and fast or slow and wheezing, unidentifiable with any of the characters. They indicate climbing a ladder up side of the huge Victorian building - the National Portrait Gallery - and squeezing through a tiny window that has been left open from the outside. Inside a figure drops down into the tiled old fashioned gent's toilets with a row of urinals glistening in the dark. They listen and hear the sounds of a security guards step fading into the distance.

NARRATOR: Alright, we weren't quite sure how to do this bit so, well this is it. Right, it's act one scene 9. We're going to act it out for you, oh and it's two weeks later. A figure dressed in black approaches the grounds of the National Portrait Gallery.

The three thieves dressed in black run onto stage ready for the part.

NARRATOR: Possibly, or possibly not resembling the Milk Tray Man.

THIEF #1 claims the lead.

NARRATOR: Listen could we get someone a bit taller?

THIEF #1 stops, looks to the narrator and THIEF #2 two takes the lead

43

NARRATOR: Someone a little slimmer?'

THIEF #3 takes the lead:

NARRATOR: I suppose that'll have to do. - The figure climbs onto a nearby parking meter.

NARRATOR: And hurdles the wall. He squeezes through an open window. *(beat)*

A small open window. *(beat)*

It was a very tiny window.

THIEF #3 makes to discard the window in disdain.

NARRATOR: Alright! He climbs through the window...and drops down *(beat)* into the gents' toilet.

THIEF #3 shakes water from his foot

NARRATOR: He hears the security guard.

They hide behind one another, they look about.

NARRATOR: Offstage a cockney voice shouts "I'm off for me break Sid".

They tuck back in before...

NARRATOR: He leaves the bathroom.

THIEF #2 pushes THIEF #3 out into the corridor

NARRATOR: It was dark.

THIEF #3 strains to see.

NARRATOR: I said it was dark.

44

THIEF #3 squints.

NARRATOR: A lot darker!

THIEF #3 covers his eyes.

NARRATOR: And so the figure began to feel his way along the corridor which was lined with pictures hanging from the walls.

The other paintings - held by THIEF #1 and THIEF #2 are summoned in.

NARRATOR: He fingers the frames of the out of work actors - I mean important artworks that line the entrance to the main gallery. He explores every inch of the pictures.

THIEF #3 works his way through the corridor and touches the different paintings and interacts with the actors until touching intimately THIEF #2. They scuffle.

NARRATOR: He enters the room.

THIEF #2 and THIEF#3 are still arguing.

NARRATOR: I said, he enters the room. *(Beat)* Enter the room!

THIEF #3 gets into position.

NARRATOR: The Duke waits in the distance.

THIEF #3 is about to walk across the front of the stage.

NARRATOR: Stop! A trap of infrared rays protects the painting.

THIEF #1 and THIEF #2bring umbrellas from the coat stand. Thief #2 swipes and THIEF #3 rolls underneath.

NARRATOR: But like erm a world class ballerina.

They attempt ballet.

NARRATOR: No not like that, more like a crowd-pleasing acrobat.

They attempt acrobatics.

NARRATOR: No no no, like…

They chase the narrator until the narrator surrenders.

NARRATOR: OK OK OK. He erm, skilfully, almost inexplicably well, as if rehearsed many times before, avoids each laser beam and balances along a high beam edge until he stands face to face with the painting.

THIEF #3 picks up the painting and makes his escape into the audience.

NARRATOR: The figure then exits. Sorry not that exit.

THIEF #3 stops. Runs to opposite aisle and asks the audience to pass the painting along. And pass it up to him climbing out at the top.

An alarm sounds and a sign pops up on stage:

'THE INTERVAL'

Lights up - Interval

ACT II

Scene 1

August 22nd 1961

On the TV - a picture of the Duke of Wellington by Goya fills the screen.

RUSSELL: The world-famous Goya portrait of the Duke of Wellington has been stolen from the National Portrait Gallery in London.

Just weeks ago, the Government paid £140,000 to rescue the masterpiece for the nation from an American oil billionaire and put it on show here at the National Portrait Gallery. This morning, it had apparently vanished into thin air.

Whoever took it went through locked doors, outwitted a team of security guards and avoided electronic security beams.

This is the first theft in the 137-year-old history of the gallery and it has happened 50 years to the date that the Mona Lisa was stolen from the Louvre Paris. Like that case, it could be a practical joke. Detectives want anyone with information to get in touch with New Scotland Yard.

Blackout

ACT II

Scene 3

September 1961. The Buntons' living room.

KEMPTON *(creeps about cautiously, looks around, as if checking no-one is about, opens the cupboard door. Pulls out a flat package from under a pile of boxes)*: Now let's have a look in the daylight - let's see what all the fuss is about.

(He holds up the painting to the light (and so that the audience can see) - it is the missing Goya portrait.)

> Not much damage...

(He notices the eyes of the portrait and is visibly taken aback).

> Actually more like a rabbit in the headlights than an Iron Duke. What was going on in your head when they painted this? You look a bit like I feel.

JOHN enters. KEMPTON drops the picture.

JOHN: What are you doing with that?

KEMPTON: Nothing, just checking it was ok...

JOHN: You weren't talking to it were you?

KEMPTON: Why would I talk to a painting? I was talking to myself. Never been saner.

JOHN: What are you going to do now Dad?

KEMPTON: This is the masterstroke, John. I'll send an anonymous note telling them they can have the painting back - all I want in exchange is a nice, large cheque - made out to the TV For the Aged

Fund.

JOHN: Dad, you can't do that.

KEMPTON: Why not?

JOHN: It's obvious isn't it - if you ask for money for the fund - they'll know it's you then.

KEMPTON: How?

JOHN: Who else is raising money for old people's TV licences?

KEMPTON: Ah. Slight rethink required then.

JOHN: It said in the paper there's a five-thousand-pound reward. They must be desperate.

KEMPTON: Pah - buttons. They don't know who they're dealing with.

JOHN: Dad, just sort it out. And get it back in the cupboard before me Mam gets back.

JOHN exits. KEMPTON puts his head in his hands. DUKE enters, stands stage left.

DUKE: Thou low-born wretch. I'll break thee for this.

KEMPTON *(to the painting):* And you can shut up as well!

DUKE: You don't even have a strategy, do you?

KEMPTON *(still talking to the painting):* A what?

DUKE: A plan - a battle plan. The whole art of war consists in getting at what is on the other side of the hill.

49

KEMPTON: What hill?

DUKE: All the business of war, and indeed the business of life, is to endeavour to find out what you don't know by what you do; that's what I call guessing at what is at the other side of the hill.

KEMPTON: Duke at this moment I am pretty sure that what's on the other side is Arthur's Hill and I've no wish to be back there.

He starts to put the painting away.

DUKE: They say I said that the battle of Waterloo was won on the playing fields of Eton. Like you I've suffered from being misquoted. Our army was composed of the scum of the earth - and a good job too. They had more about them than any public schoolboys - and they terrified the enemy.

KEMPTON: I've got a letter to write.

DUKE: You know what else I said.

KEMPTON: What?

DUKE: Publish and be damned.

KEMPTON, realising he's talking to himself, bundles the painting back into the cupboard.

Blackout

ACT II

Scene 4

Scotland Yard

DET INSP. MATTHEW HOMES of the Yard and DET CONST, MIKE STEVENS are discussing the case.

DI HOMES: What've we got Stevens? Ten days in and we need something new for the press.

DC STEVEN: And the Commander. But we can't handle any more cranks and reward chasers - do you not think this is one for Interpol now Sir?

DI HOMES: We are not bringing that bunch of bumbling idiots into my case Stevens.

DC STEVEN (*looking in his notebook*): We've had 100 detectives on the case. We've searched 150 rooms, 250 windows, 40 doors. Interviewed 20 security guards, 60 gallery workers, 100 contractors and 6000 members of the public. Sir.

DI HOMES: And still no clue of the modus operandi, never mind the motive.

DC STEVEN: Sir, is this some sort of criminal mastermind?

DI HOMES: And why would a criminal mastermind want that particular painting DC Stevens? There's more to this than financial gain, mark my words.

DC STEVEN: The gallery director's tearing his hair out - he's on the phone every hour. Sir.

DI HOMES: Have you got anything to tell me?

DC STEVEN: Just two sets of footprints in the builder's compound. Sir.

DI HOMES (*looking at the map on the wall*): So, we reckon there were at least two of them. Probably young and fit, light on their feet to dodge all the beams. Clever too. They must have cased the joint for days, come in in opening hours, picked the right moment, hid the thing somewhere until the coast was clear. They had probably concealed themselves inside after the doors were locked. They took the picture out through the men's lavatory at the back, crept through two courtyards, and shinned over the wall by the back gates. Probably cheeky enough to use the Ministry of Work's ladders to get it away around the back. Presume it wasn't lit round there. But... why the Iron Duke?

Phone rings...

DC STEVEN (*picks up the phone*): Scotland Yard, DC Stevens. *(Nodding to confirm with DI):* No, no press statements. Tell the reporters we'll be in touch when we have something to say. *(Pause)*Ah. In that case, yes, we will speak to them.

(DI HOMES is shaking his head, pointing to cut off at throat)

Put him through.

DC STEVEN (*puts hand over receiver*): It's Reuter's news agency Sir. They say they've got a ransom letter for the Duke.

DI HOMES: Another hoax.

DC STEVEN (*back on phone*): Ok, yes, so it definitely says the framer is F Gallais and Son and 1958 on the back? And he wants £140,000? And a free pardon?

DI HOMES (*grabs phone*): Go on. *(to Stevens)* Take this down Stevens. *(Back to the phone)* It's for ransom, to be given to a charity? And it says what? None of this group has criminal convictions? Get that letter here immediately. And don't publish anything until we issue a formal statement. There's no reason to get excited. It's probably another hoax.

(Puts phone down.)

DC STEVEN: Hmm, either a complete crank or it could be real.

DI HOMES: Of course it's real. This is not your normal criminal. It's someone with a grudge - demanding just the price of the painting. A blackmailer would have threatened to destroy it if we didn't pay up. No, it's someone with a, a cause.

DC STEVEN: So what do we do now?

DI HOMES: We have another cup of tea. And we wait.

They exit.

Blackout

ACT II

Scene 5

One year later, at the Odeon Cinema in Newcastle,
September1962.

*KEMPTON and DOTTY walk into the audience, into a row near
the front. A large screen on the stage shows the feature film is
about to start. KEMPTON and DOTTY are sitting sharing a bag
of toffees waiting for the film to start.*

DOTTY: I'm so pleased you said you'd come tonight love.
                 I can't wait to see this film - everybody's talking
                 about it.

KEMPTON: It's not my type of thing - I prefer a good
                 documentary.

DOTTY: Oh can you not just try to enjoy yourself for
                 once? It might take you out of yourself for a bit -
                 get you out of your black mood.

KEMPTON: Alright, it's just I need a job not an hour in a
                 darkened room with the bright stars of
                 Hollywood...

DOTTY: Shush - it might give you some ideas for your
                 plays. Shush, it's starting.

*KEMPTON accepts a toffee from DOTTY and puts it in his mouth.
They settle down to watch the film. The film begins with the music,
fades as if being fast forwarded and then plays the section at Dr
No's mansion where James Bond (Sean Connery) walks up the
stairs past a painting on an easel - the Goya painting of the Duke
of Wellington - and says or looks as if to say "Ah that's where it
went." Kempton splutters on the toffee, starts coughing and tries
to squeeze up and push past to get out. DOTTY is embarrassed.*

54

DOTTY: Shhhh. What're you doing - just sit down and shut up. Have another black bullet.

KEMPTON, still spluttering, stomps out along the row and out of the cinema, back to the stage - his front room. DOTTY follows, apologising.

The screen fades. The Bunton's living room - JOHN enters.

KEMPTON and JOHN sit at table, reading papers. Kempton absorbed in the Daily Mirror.

JOHN: You didn't enjoy the film then?

KEMPTON: Load of rubbish.

JOHN: Dad, stop it. I've seen it. I went with Angie. I couldn't believe it. Me stomach just flipped over - I thought I was going to be sick.

KEMPTON: Forget it John. Just put it out of your mind.

JOHN: But Dad, what are we going to do about it? There's been nothing since you sent that note. And then it turns up in Dr No's mansion for flippin' heck's sake.

KEMPTON: John - we're family. We look after each other. You have to promise me you will never say anything.

JOHN: Dad! It's doing me head in. I've been thinking about what you said. I am joining up. What are we going to do?

KEMPTON: I am going to bide my time.

DOTTY enters, with shopping - puts it on table. Cucumber sticking out of shopping basket.

55

DOTTY: Bide your time for what?

JOHN: I'm just saying Mam, I'm sick of driving about going nowhere in me job. I'm leaving.

DOTTY: No need to be hasty pet.

JOHN: You might as well know I've already done it. I've signed up for the Durhams. I'm going tomorrow.

DOTTY: Our John! You know nothing about being in the army. You could end up anywhere. Tell him Kempton, tell him, he's got a good job here.

KEMPTON: It's his decision Dotty.

DOTTY: What! You! What have you been saying to him? What've you filled his head with now? How could you?

She grabs the cucumber and brandishes it at Kempton.

KEMPTON *(calm):* It's up to him. Probably for the best. Can you put the salad down please?

DOTTY: John - what does Angie say?

JOHN: It's not about her Mam - I've just got to get a life that's away from here.

DOTTY: So it's my fault now? (*She throws the cucumber down.*) This family's falling apart. I'm... I'm... going to our Linda's.

She picks up the handbag, storms out.

KEMPTON: Are you sure son?

56

JOHN:	Dad I'll go mad if I stay here.
KEMPTON:	Ok lad.
JOHN:	I just wish I could get it out of my head.
KEMPTON:	You are not involved in this John.
JOHN:	But...
KEMPTON:	This is all entirely my doing, my campaign, my problem. I'll take the blame - or I'll take the credit. Now, swear John. Swear on your mother's life you won't tell anyone.
JOHN:	Dad I can't...
KEMPTON:	Swear! Now...
JOHN:	Ok, ok, I promise.

He leaves. KEMPTON looks at the cupboard and back to the door. Stares ahead.

Blackout

ACT II

Scene 6

Scotland Yard a couple of days later, July 3 1962.

DC Steven and DI Homes at desk. Newspapers on the table.

DI HOMES: Another note Stevens?

DC STEVEN *(reading note):* Yes Sir, and this time he's sent the label from the back. Says the Duke is safe, "his temperature cared for - his future uncertain." He wants a pardon or the right to leave the country - "banishment" he says.

And that some "nonconformist type with the fearless fortitude of a Montgomery starts the fund *(looks up from reading)* - whatever that is - for £140,000. No law can touch him. Propriety may frown - but God must smile...." It's very weird English Sir.

DI HOMES: Bizarre. He's an eccentric alright. But he's got the painting. And we have no idea where he is.

DC STEVEN: What now? Get the psychiatrists in again?

DI HOMES: I think a cup of tea will prove more fruitful than all that voodoo in these circumstances. We'll do nothing. We will wait.

Music – The Man from Laramie, by Jimmy Young.

Blackout

ACT II

Scene 7

A year later. Still in Scotland Yard - 1963.

Lights up. The pile of newspapers on the table has grown higher.

DC STEVEN: Sir! Another note. But you're not going to like this one.

DI HOMES: Give it here. (*He reads...*) "The Yard are looking for a needle in a haystack, but they haven't a clue where the haystack is... I am offering three penn'orth of old Spanish firewood in exchange for £140,000 of human happiness. An amnesty would not be out of order". The cheeky bastard.

And he just suggests as an afterthought that all the national newspapers should give five bob for every thousand copies they sell with the story in it - and then he'll return the Duke! Who the hell does he think he is?

He sits down.

DC STEVEN (*checking notebook*): He's an intelligent, imaginative man with a strong moral sense, but now, a guilty conscience as well.

DI HOMES: Maybe what he thinks is a magnificent gesture will ultimately eat away at him until he eventually gives himself up. Or he'll get so frustrated that he'll just get rid - destroy - the painting. Then we're all buggered Stevens.

DC STEVEN: The papers are making a meal out of it.

59

DI HOMES (*angrily gesturing at the pile of newspapers*): Yes - at our bloody expense Stevens. We look like fools.

DC STEVEN: Not as bad as the Gallery director though. He looks a right idiot.

DI HOMES: He didn't deserve to run an art gallery - he couldn't run a bath!

DC STEVEN: So, what now. Shall we tell the press we're ready to talk terms with him?

DI HOMES: No.

DC STEVEN: Cup of tea?

DI HOMES: Let's make it a pint.

DC STEVEN: And?

DC STEVEN and **DI HOMES** (*together*): We wait.

Blackout

ACT II

Scene 8

The Bunton's living room two years on - early 1965.

DOTTY is in the kitchen, coat and headscarf on as if ready for travelling; luggage near her feet.

Music: The Leader of the Pack by the Shangri-Las is playing.

KEMPTON *(enters)*: You're off to your Linda's again, are you?

DOTTY: No. I'm going to Portsmouth. For a while.

KEMPTON: To see Celia? Ok - I'll manage.

DOTTY: Kempton, please listen to me. I've tried and tried but it's not working is it.

KEMPTON: What's not working?

DOTTY: This. This family. You and me. Ever since you went to prison all you do is write and sit around thinking. And since our John went away it's been worse. For four years now Kempton and nothing's changing.

KEMPTON: Is it my fault if the BBC's got no idea what good writing is when they see it?

DOTTY: And you're obsessed with the papers and the news... it's getting on my nerves.

(She goes to switch off the news on the TV)

KEMPTON: Don't switch it off...

DOTTY: See - when I say anything you bite my head off. I feel like my life has stopped - and I'm going to do something about it.

KEMPTON: What?

DOTTY: Let me put it in plain English. I'm leaving you. I'm going to see Celia and when I come back, I'm staying with our Linda. There's food in the pantry and I've left the rent book on the shelf. I've paid the paper bill - and the television licence as well.

KEMPTON displays no reaction.

DOTTY: If you need anything am sure your sister will help. And - if our John does get in touch, tell him where I am will you?

She exits.

Music: Leader of Pack plays louder then fades.

DUKE *enters. (pause)*: Your son enlisted then.

KEMPTON (*startled*): Don't do that!

DUKE: And your wife is gone. What's your plan Kempton?

KEMPTON: To do the right thing. Like them.

DUKE: Ha - people talk of enlisting to satisfy some fine military feeling. No such thing. Our men enlisted from having got bastard children - some for minor offences – many more for drink.

KEMPTON: Yes, they were all escaping something.

DUKE: So?

KEMPTON: I need to think. Need to work out what's on the other side of that hill.

DUKE: It's all about timing - and communication. It's been two years - Let them know you're still here. "Up Guards and at 'em!"

KEMPTON: It's going to be a bitter victory.

DUKE: You better get on with it man. My rule was always to do the business of the day in the day. You've waited too long already.

KEMPTON: But get on with what? I don't know how to get over that hill - without being taken prisoner.

DUKE: In the end, it's all about who pounds the hardest. But maybe you're not the pounding type. Perhaps it's time to use some psychology. Appeal to their better nature. Write this down. *(dictating)* - I know that I am in the wrong.

KEMPTON *(writing in his notebook)*: What?!

DUKE: The hardest thing of all for a soldier is to retreat...

KEMPTON: Hmm. *(writing)* I know that I am in the wrong... but I have gone too far to retreat.

DUKE *(still dictating):* Liberty was risked in what I mistakenly thought was a magnificent gesture - all to no purpose so far.

KEMPTON (*Nods towards the Duke*): I feel the time has come to make one final effort.

DUKE: Up Guards and at 'em.

Blackout

63

ACT II

Scene 9

Scotland Yard, a few days later. *DC STEVENS and DI HOMES are reading the letter.*

DI HOMES: "...I propose to return the painting anonymously if the following plan is agreed." Oh here we go another great idea...

DS STEVEN: "The portrait to be put on private exhibition at a five-shilling view fee for a month, after which it would be returned to the gallery. A collection box to be placed at the side of picture for good people to give if so inclined. The affair to be a true charity and all moneys collected, minus nothing for expenses given to the place I name...

DI HOMES: What the heck is his agenda?

DC STEVEN: "... The matter to end there - no prosecutions - no police enquiries as to who has committed this awful deed. I do not think the authorities need fear the feat being emulated by others - the risk is great - the material reward nil." Yer bugger...

DI HOMES: I hope he has not done to the Goya masterpiece what he has done to the English language.

DC STEVEN: What?

DI HOMES: Massacred it.

DC STEVEN: Do you think the Gallery might agree to this one Sir?

DI HOMES: It's not the gallery now Stevens, it's the

Government. And we need to be careful. If he gets too frustrated he might end up destroying the picture. We've waited long enough. Time to call for reinforcements.

DC STEVEN (*picking up phone*): I'll call Interpol Sir.

DI HOMES: No. No. It's time to enlist our friends - the gentlemen of the press. *(He picks up the phone)* Homes of Scotland Yard here. Get your Chief Reporter round here double quick.

BILL *flies through the door, now wearing a press style mac and hat...*

DI HOMES: And you are...

BILL: Bill Chester, assistant to the Assistant Chief Reporter.

DI HOMES: How long have you been on the Mirror?

BILL: I've just started - I finished me training in Newcastle and managed to get this job straightaway.

DI HOMES: Oh great they've sent the trainee. And he's a Geordie. Where's your whippet lad?

BILL: Eh? Ah, ha ha, don't worry. I've done a lot of national stuff. You can see my by-line in the Mirror a lot now - once already this year. And I've been covering Bow Street Magistrates - some great tales in there...

DI HOMES: Does your boss know what he's doing sending you? This is a big story and I need you to do exactly as I say. You've heard of Goya?

BILL: Em Spanish?

DI HOMES: Yes...

BILL: The bullfighter was he... killed the little white bull....

DI STEVEN: No he was a painter. Who painted a very famous portrait of a very famous General, called the Duke of Wellington.

BILL: The one that was in Dr No?

DI STEVEN: Spot on. It's been held for ransom since 1961. And we need it back. And the crank that's got it behind bars.

BILL: Is he dangerous?

DI HOMES: Only if you were hoping to be in Her Majesty's New Year's Honours List.

BILL: What's the painting worth?

DI HOMES: Priceless. It didn't just cost 140 grand; you can't put a price on the embarrassment it's caused the Government and the art establishment...

BILL: And the police?

DI HOMES: Chester - here's your elusive exclusive. Print this crank's ...letter... in full. Next - and now make sure you get all this down - on your front page ask our *loquacious* thief to return the Goya to the Mirror...

BILL *struggles to get it all down.*

DI HOMES: ...loquacious - it means wordy - tell him to

66

deposit the painting in a safe place of his choice and then let the Mirror Editor in Holburn Circus know where it can be found.

BILL: Fantastic, thanks, Matt, em, I'm sure we can do that.

DI HOMES: Wait, here is the important part. The Daily Mirror will offer in return to hire a hall where the painting could be exhibited for the benefit of any harity nominated by the present possessor. Have you got that?

BILL: Yes. So just to get this straight, you want us to help you catch this thief by offering him a free exhibition and a chance to make more money?

DI HOMES: That's right. So, Alan Price, you tell your Editor to give me a call if he's got any problems with that.

BILL: And does that mean we can say he won't be prosecuted - he can just give the painting back, get some cash for his charity and walk away, scot-free...

DI HOMES: You can't guarantee him immunity from prosecution Chester. But you don't need to make a great deal of that do you?

BILL: So, but, Matt, Inspector, we're not really going to do all that for him are we?

DI HOMES *(sarcastic....)*: Oh absolutely. If you strike a bargain you must stick to your end of it.

Blackout

ACT II

Scene 10

A desk in the newsroom of the Daily Mirror.   The desk has a heavy old typewriter and a spike - full.

Music: The Who - Won't Get Fooled Again...

BILL (*picks up the telephone and dials*): Scotland Yard please. DC Stevens? Aye, hello there, it's Bill Chester from the Daily Mirror speaking. Yes, something to report - we've had a letter in the post. Says he'll return the picture if we put it on show and raise £30,000 for charity. I'm assuming it's a he mind, you don't think it's a woman do you?

(holds phone away from his ear)

> Anyway, he says he wants us to make it obvious in the personal column, and we have to put in a message, signed with the name Whitfield. Is that name significant by the way?

> No? Ok, it appears that if we do what he says, we'll get a letter telling us where to pick up the Goya.

> Right. Yes. That'll be in the personal column tomorrow. Is there anything else I can do for you? No, I've told you I haven't got a whippet. And Constable, Alan Price was from Jarrow, not North Shields.

> Yes… I'll call you if I hear anything else. Don't forget it's my exclusive mind. Turrah now.

Blackout

68

ACT II

Scene 11

The Bunton's kitchen (April 1965)

KEMPTON has the painting out on the table. He's opening out of its brown paper wrapping. He looks dishevelled.

KEMPTON: Here we are Duke. Finally facing my Waterloo eh? I guess we are going to find out what is over that hill. What to do next?

DOTTY enters behind him.

DOTTY: Kempton? Are you talking to that parcel?

KEMPTON: Dotty - I didn't know you were coming back.

DOTTY: I just came to see if you were ok.

KEMPTON: I'm fine … or maybe not. If I'm honest I miss you. And John.

DOTTY: John's fine. Better than. He's getting married. To Angie - you remember the girl he met at Wills.

KEMPTON: Like us then.

DOTTY: A bit. What's all this?

KEMPTON (*looking round room*): Sorry it's a bit of a mess.

DOTTY (*gesturing at painting*): I mean this.

KEMPTON (*trying to hide it*): Just an old print I found at Miller's salerooms.

DOTTY: Let's have a look. (S*he pulls the brown paper*

69

wrapping away...)

Oh my God sweet Mary mother of Jesus and I'm not even Catholic. It is isn't it. It's the painting they've been looking for. The letters to the papers... Kempton. It was you.

KEMPTON: It's not how it looks...

DOTTY: Thank God for that because to me it looks like you took yourself off to London where you've never been in your life, carried off the art crime of the century in one of the world's most secure art galleries, played cat and mouse with the top cops in the country, embarrassed only the Prime Minister, blackmailed the country for years - and now you seem to be best friends with a few dollops of paint on a bit of wood. Please tell me you didn't do this Kempton. Or not on your own, obviously.

KEMPTON: I, look, it's here isn't it.

DOTTY: No, tell me you did do it yourself. Because I've got a horrible feeling. Tell me this was nothing to do with our John?

KEMPTON: No, no, no, it has nothing to do with John. And strange as it may seem, Dotty, it is all my doing. I spent a lot of time working it all out. And it feels strangely good to be able to confess this to you.

DOTTY: Why? Was it for the reward?

KEMPTON (*smiles, beams*): Of course not. For the TV licences.

70

DOTTY: Ah no! And you couldn't even get publicity for your campaign could you. You should have told me – we could have sorted it out together. Were you talking to him - it - when I came in?

KEMPTON: No, of course not.... But it has been a bit solitary without you.

DOTTY: Bloody hell. I'd rather have been ditched for another woman. Instead it's another man. And he's 200-years-old and made of paint.

DOTTY, speechless, stomps out.

KEMPTON: Dotty - I can explain.

DUKE *enters:* Terrifying isn't she.

KEMPTON (*resigned*): Yes. Very.

DUKE: The only thing I was ever afraid of is fear. So I suggest this... take courage and put your faith in this helping hand that's been offered - let's face it, it's Hobson's choice. You can't live with me; you can't live without me. You can't destroy me but you can't keep me.

KEMPTON: So now is the right time - I'll take their "sporting offer".

DUKE: Wise people learn when they can; fools learn when they must. Your fight goes on - on your terms. You don't need me anymore.

KEMPTON: This will be the last battle of our campaign together Duke. You're off to Birmingham tomorrow.

DUKE: Up Guards - and at 'em!

KEMPTON (*sticks the paper back down over the picture making a parcel):* He never said that really.

Blackout

ACT II

Scene 12

May 21 1965

Scotland Yard – DI HOMES is at his desk.

DC STEVEN (*enters and places the brown paper parcel on the desk*):   Left luggage office at New Street Railway Station, Birmingham. He's a Brummie!

DI HOMES: I wouldn't be so sure. Let's see what we have here.

He opens the parcel.

DC STEVEN: Is this it?

DI HOMES (*almost showing some excitement*):   It looks like the real thing to me. It had been there for two weeks? We're hot on the trail again then. Is there a description of who left it?

DC STEVEN (*checking the notebook*):   Apparently someone aged about 20, Caucasian male, medium height, slim, in a blue duffel coat. The baggage clerk said he was well spoken, with bushy hair. Gave his name as Mr Bloxham and paid his shilling fee. The clerk remembered he said "be very careful with this" when he handed it over.

DI HOMES: Mr Bloxham eh?

DC STEVEN: Is that significant?

DI HOMES: Maybe. Get an identikit and his description out. And check whether anyone's claimed the reward.

They both linger, inspecting the painting closely.

DC STEVEN: Boss, where's its frame?

DI HOMES: That's not important - it's the painting we need - but it seems none the worse for wear. I expect he went through worse on the battlefields of Europe... Let's get it back and on show where it belongs!

DC STEVEN: And shall I call Mr Scoop Chester to give him his exclusive then?

DI HOMES: Bugger that Stevens. Get the BBC. We're having a full-scale press conference.

Blackout

ACT II

Scene 13

Two weeks later. The Bunton's living room.

Music: Painted Black by the Rolling Stones. KEMPTON is at the table, with the Daily Mirror.

KEMPTON: I've been betrayed - by the great institution of the British Press. I will have the final say though. Whether they'll print it is another matter.

He picks up the typewriter and starts typing.

Property has won - charity has lost. Indeed a black day for journalism. We took the Goya in sporting endeavour (addressing the newspaper) - you Mr Editor pinched it back by a broken promise. You furthermore have the effrontery to pat yourself on the back in your triumph.

If you think I will take your advice to vanish from contemporary history you are mistaken. But you will have to wait for my next - and final - move. I'm going over the top. *(pause)*

And then I'm going to stop talking to myself.

Music: Paint It Black by the Rolling Stones

DOTTY *(enters, rushing in):* Kempton, I have to tell you something.

KEMPTON: Are you coming back?

DOTTY: No! I've had to leave the Bingo.

KEMPTON: Did they throw you out?

DOTTY: Kempton! Linda says John's told his brother.

KEMPTON: What?

DOTTY: And now Ken's told his pal.

KEMPTON: Who?

DOTTY: I don't know…

KEMPTON: How?

DOTTY: Who cares – they must've both had a drink. We need to find them.

KEMPTON: Why?

DOTTY: Because this pal says he's going to go for the reward.

KEMPTON: What?

DOTTY: What are we going to do? They say they'll go to the police.

KEMPTON: Nobody does that to our family. If the old folk don't benefit, nobody gets that money.

He grabs his coat and they both exit.

Blackout

ACT II

Scene 14

Scotland Yard, July 1965.

DC STEVENS and DI HOMES engrossed at their desk.
KEMPTON *enters carrying a pile of tattered brown card files.*

KEMPTON: DI Homes? I am turning myself in for the Goya.

The officers are startled, one almost falls off seat in surprise.

DI HOMES *(obviously not interested):* Get some details Stevens.

KEMPTON: Bunton. Kempton Bunton.

DC STEVENS *(trying not to laugh):* Sorry Sir, are you saying
that it was you who stole the Goya?

KEMPTON: Yes. It was me.

DC STEVEN: Mr Bunton, believe it or not a lot of people have
told us they stole the painting. But they didn't.
Now, would you like a cup of tea?

KEMPTON: I'm here to confess. I committed no crime but I
took the Goya and I returned the Goya. Now, are
you going to charge me?

DC STEVEN: One thing at a time Mr Bunton. Where you from?
Newcastle?

KEMPTON *(bringing out handwritten sheaves of paper from the
files):* How could you tell? I've already written a
statement to save you the bother and here are my
operational files describing how each manoeuvre
was planned and executed.

77

DI HOMES (*interrupting, slightly irritated*):   Slight problem, Mr Bunton. We think there were two men who committed this crime. And if you don't mind my saying, you don't exactly match the description of a daredevil cat burglar with the build of an athlete, the training of a stunt man, and the mind of a master criminal....

KEMPTON: Since no one saw me it's unlikely you'll have an accurate description.

DI HOMES: Mr Bunton since you're so insistent, let's get on with it. Where did you say you live?

KEMPTON: Newcastle. Benwell to be exact.

DC STEVEN: Where's that - Scotland?

KEMPTON (*getting irritated*):   No.

DI HOMES: Stevens, call the Newcastle copshop.

KEMPTON: Yewcroft Avenue, Newcastle upon Tyne in the North East of England. Where I can walk to the end of my street and look down on the magnificent River Tyne - the backbone of industry - and see where my Geordie colleagues are building at Swan Hunters the greatest warships ever seen - that have kept this country safe - at Armstrong's where the tanks are rolling off the production line as fast as our armies go to pointless war.

And at Rolls Royce, where they are building the world's finest engines for our country's fleet of aeroplanes.

We are not the types to be daunted by the simple

challenge of slipping a picture painted on an old bit of firewood from under the noses of some dozy guards.

DC STEVEN *(from the phone)*: Seems he has got form Sir.

DI HOMES: Alright, Mr Bunton let's just go over the details here. When did you steal the portrait?

KEMPTON: Nineteen sixty-one. The twenty first of August. It's all in there.

DI HOMES: What day of the week was that?

KEMPTON: Monday... yes Monday.

DI HOMES: Are you sure?

KEMPTON: I think so.

DI HOMES: What time was it?

KEMPTON: Five fifty, or thereabouts.

DI HOMES: Was it dark at the time?

KEMPTON: A bit.

DI HOMES: As far as I know, it wasn't dark at the time. Are you telling me the truth?

KEMPTON: It's a long time ago. I'm fairly sure.

DI HOMES: Where did you take it from?

KEMPTON: Opposite the main door entrance.

DC STEVEN: How did you get past the infrared beams?

KEMPTON: I just kept my head down.

DC STEVEN: How did you get out?

EMPTON: Through the toilet window and over a wall.

DI HOMES: Mr Bunton, how much do you weigh?

KEMPTON: Pardon?

DI HOMES: What's your weight?

KEMPTON: I don't know maybe twelve, thirteen stones?

DI HOMES *(looking sceptical):* And when was the last time you ran for a bus?

KEMPTON: I'm never late so not that often, you're right.

DI HOMES: Were you by yourself?

KEMPTON *(emphatically)*: Yes.

DI HOMES: Why did you steal it?

KEMPTON: To ransom it. I thought there would be a big collection straight away for it if it was that important.

DC STEVEN: How did you get to London from Newcastle?

KEMPTON: I hitchhiked on trucks.

DC STEVEN: Where did you stay?

KEMPTON: Lodgings at Wembley.

DI HOMES: Mr Bunton how much do you get on the dole?

KEMPTON: Eight pounds six shillings.

DI HOMES: So how did you afford to come to London?

KEMPTON: I only had ninepence in my pocket. One spot of luck though - I bumped into a cousin who'd been away to sea for years. He was only too pleased to lend me a tenner.

DI HOMES: A very fortunate coincidence. What happened when you went to the Gallery?

KEMPTON: I saw the crowds and all the guards and I knew I had a challenge. I cased the joint - if I can put it that way - and spotted the back way in and out.

DC STEVEN: How did you reach to see out of the gents' lavatory window?

KEMPTON: I had to stand on the toilet bowl.

DC STEVEN: What did you do next?

KEMPTON: I boobed the window and the cubicle door.

DI HOMES: "Boobed" them?

KEMPTON: I wedged a twist of paper into the window catch. Then I went and bought some cellophane and stuck it across the door lock. I went back the next day and they were still there so I knew it was a fair bet they would not be touched.

DI HOMES: What else did you do?

KEMPTON: Reconnoitre. I talked to the guards - it was easy to find out their shift patterns and where the beams were. They told me what time the cleaners came in and they don't set off the alarms.

DC STEVEN: How did you get the gallery painting away?

KEMPTON: I had to borrow a car.

DC STEVEN: Borrow?

KEMPTON: Yes when I couldn't find one with the keys in the ignition I was almost going to go straight back to King's Cross. I knew I'd need a car to get the painting away. But then I saw a man stagger from his car as if drunk. He'd left the keys in the ignition. I just slipped it away. And took it back after.

DI HOMES: Are you admitting car theft as well Mr Bunton?

KEMPTON: No, I returned it intact apart from half a gallon of petrol which no doubt he would not have noticed and in any event probably saved him from a greater crime of driving while incapable.

DC STEVEN: And where did you park the car?

KEMPTON: On Orange Street at the back.

DC STEVEN: Then what?

KEMPTON: I climbed onto the car to get over the wall, picked up the ladder on the other side and made my way across the compound. I propped it up and climbed up to the lavatory window. I manoeuvred myself through the window and then quickly made my way through avoiding all the beams to reach the painting and lift it. That's all.

DC STEVEN: You put on a bit of weight since then, then? And you went straight back to the lodgings in Wembley.

DI HOMES: Where did you put the painting?

KEMPTON: Under the bed.

DI HOMES: Why?

KEMPTON: I left it there, and came back a couple of weeks later to retrieve it, after the fuss died down.

DI HOMES: How did you know it would still be there?

KEMPTON: Have you seen the state of those lodgings – no chance of a cleaner going under the bed.

DI HOMES: What did you do with the frame?

KEMPTON: I've told you I can't remember.

DC STEVEN: Who is Mr Bloxham?

KEMPTON: Who?

DC STEVEN: Your accomplice Mr Bunton. The man who deposited the painting at Birmingham New Street left luggage office. Where is he?

KEMPTON: He doesn't exist. There is nobody in this story but me.

DC STEVEN: Nobody? What about your wife?

KEMPTON: She knew nothing of this. Most of the time she was away or indisposed.

DC STEVEN: What did she make of all your comings and goings?

KEMPTON: I - I told her I'd gone fishing.

DC STEVEN: She believed you I suppose.

KEMPTON: I always lied satisfactorily to Mrs B. I had a secret to keep and you just can't trust a gossipy woman, bless her heart.

DI HOMES (*getting exasperated*): Right that's it. Kempton Bunton, you are under arrest for the theft of a painting by Francisco Goya belonging to the Trustees of the National Portrait Gallery; the theft of a gold painted frame belonging to same such Trustees; demanding money with menaces from Lord Robbins, Chairman of the Trustees of the National Gallery, demanding money with menaces from Mr Lee Howard, the Editor of the Daily Mirror, and ...

KEMPTON: Yes?

DI HOMES: Causing a Public Nuisance. You do not have to say anything however it may harm your defence if you do not mention when questioned something which you later rely on in court. Anything you do say may be given in evidence. Take him down Stevens.

KEMPTON (*standing up*): Not guilty. The case will get thrown out you know. Where there is no criminal intent there can be no conviction.

DC STEVEN: Come on Mr Bunton. You can phone your wife from the cells.

KEMPTON (*suddenly exhausted*): No, but have you got a pen and paper? I've got a letter to write.

Blackout

ACT II

Scene 15

Office of the Daily Mirror.

Background Music – Walk Don't Run – The Voyagers

BILL *(reading a letter):* For the attention of Bill Chester, Daily Mirror, Fleet Street. I have reached the zenith of my campaign – let's hope it is not the nadir.

Finally I will be heard, and when I am, I will not forget those who have been the trusted allies of my campaign. Betrayed by the fourth estate - the press - failed by family, and in the matter of my good wife, I am lucky if I am in the dog house.

I have one last favour I can bestow. Be at the Old Bailey tomorrow at ten am and finally, you will have your "elusive exclusive."

You may need your Essential Law for Journalists.

My thanks to you Bill.

Blackout

85

ACT II

Scene 16

The Old Bailey, London, November 4, 1965.

KEMPTON is in the dock. His suit is shabby; his (balding) hair is smoothed down, he is impassive, shows no emotion. John is sitting watching, in his military uniform. Bill is sitting in the press box, notebook ready. The Recorder of London, JUDGE CARL AARVOLD presides. JUDGE AARVOLD beckons JEREMY HUTCHINSON QC to the bench.

OS: Court stand!

JUDGE: Before we start, I dismiss the charge of causing a public nuisance. Please be seated. Mr Hutchinson?

QC: Your honour, this case is unique. It tests the fundamental of the law of theft. It requires us not to test whether Mr Bunton took the painting or not - he admits he did - there is no question of that - but whether this was against the law of larceny - or not.

I contend that it was not. Mr Bunton took the picture in order to bring attention to a very important point.

He did not take it with the intention of depriving its owner.

Mr Bunton is clearly an idealist, an idealist with a moral conscience who became enraged because the government refused to exempt old-age

86

pensioners from paying their TV licence fees. He refused to pay for his licence and in 1960 he twice chose prison rather than pay the fine.

Then he heard about the purchase of the Goya and again he felt very strongly about that. Here is a country that can afford £140,000 for a picture, and they are not prepared to spend any money on free television licences for old age pensioners.

So he planned the burglary.

Mr Bunton was your object to steal the portrait from the National Gallery in revenge for the way you had been treated by the authorities over your television licence?

KEMPTON: That is not correct.

QC: When you walked out of the National Gallery carrying the portrait were you saying to yourself: I always intend to return it?

KEMPTON: It was no good to me otherwise - I would not have hung it in my kitchen!

QC: Did you ever tell your wife that you had been hiding the Goya for nearly four years?

KEMPTON: No, the world would have known if I had done so.

JUDGE: We will now take a short adjournment.

Bell rings.

Music – Rolling Stones – Bob Dylan

Characters move around the stage. KEMPTON remains in the dock. Bell rings.

87

JUDGE: Ladies and Gentlemen of the jury, you have a lot to consider. Let me sum up for you.

The defendant tells you that he managed to get in and he managed to get out. You have seen him; you know his age. So far as we know there was only one person involved in this, and the defendant tells you he was there doing it himself with no one else helping him at all.

If you accept this remarkable feat by the defendant, then there is only one question left to answer.

If you believe the defendant meant to return the painting if his ransom bid failed, then you must acquit him; if on the other hand you feel he would hang on until he got the money, you must bring in a different verdict.

The court door opens quietly and DOTTY slips in and sits down.

JUDGE: Chairman of the Jury are you ready to give your verdict?

CHAIRMAN: We are.

JUDGE: Members of the jury, on the count of demanding money with menaces from Lord Robbins, Chairman of the Trustees of the National Gallery, how do you find the defendant: guilty or not guilty?

CHAIRMAN: Not guilty.

JUDGE: On the count of demanding money with menaces from Mr Lee Howard, the Editor of the Daily Mirror, how do you find the defendant: guilty or

88

not guilty?

CHAIRMAN: Not guilty.

JUDGE: On the count of theft of a painting by Francisco Goya belonging to the Trustees of the National Portrait Gallery, how do you find the defendant: guilty or not guilty?

CHAIRMAN: Not guilty. *(Gasps of surprise in the court room)*

JUDGE: On the count of the theft of a gold painted frame valued at £100, belonging to same such Trustees, how do you find the defendant: guilty or not guilty?

CHAIRMAN: Guilty. *(More gasps of surprise from the court room audience)*

JUDGE: Quiet please. It is time to pass sentence. Motives, even if they are good, cannot justify theft, and creeping into public galleries in order to extract pictures of value so that you can use them for your own purposes has got to be discouraged. Taking all those matters into account, I can only sentence you to a short term of imprisonment of three months.

DOTTY: Oh, Kempton.

JUDGE: Take him down!

KEMPTON is taken down from the dock.

Music: When I woke up this morning... Crispian St Peter

Blackout

ACT II

Scene 17

Four years later - 1969 in the Bunton's living room.

Music: Something Stupid by Frank and Nancy Sinatra.

KEMPTON is hunched in the armchair - motionless. DOTTY is anxiously doing something with a dishcloth/apron. JOHN is standing up - distraught.

DOTTY: I thought it was all over John. I'd just gone back to Bingo. Just starting to hold me head up again. And now I find out it wasn't him! You couldn't just keep quiet? For me? For your Dad?

JOHN: I'm sorry. I'm sorry. You haven't spoken to me for years, since... It was preying on me mind - when they stopped the van I panicked.

DOTTY: You've kept quiet all this time. You must think I'm stupid. I believed you both.

JOHN: I thought I could put it right.

DOTTY: Kempton - the police'll be here soon. What are we going to do?

KEMPTON (*weary*): We'll do the right thing Dotty.

DOTTY: But what?

JOHN: Dad I don't want to go to prison. I've got Angie now. And the bairns.

KEMPTON: You should have thought of that when you threw the bloody frame away.

90

JOHN: It was really stupid. The whole thing. But I thought I was helping you. And you - you kept on sending things to the papers even when you got out of prison. Dragging it all up.

KEMPTON: It was a principle! *(He walks over and opens door)*. Welcome, Detective Inspector Homes.

DI HOMES enters.

DOTTY: Can I get you a cup of tea?

DI HOMES *(gesturing no):* I won't take long. You John Bunton are a very lucky man. And you Kempton Bunton, thanks to your tall tales you're an unreliable witness.

KEMPTON: I thought so.

DI HOMES *(pointing at John)*: There's no evidence to send you down.

Your Dad took the rap when nobody believed him - and he's the great martyr to his cause. It's just too embarrassing for her majesty's government to rake this up.

So you've won. But. If either of you or anybody in this family ever breathes a word of this we will be back. And to make sure the Home Secretary himself needs you both to sign this. *(Offers a pen to John)*.

JOHN: What is it? *(He takes the pen and signs the document)*

DI HOMES: A sort of injunction. Means you don't talk about this or any matter connected with it to anyone -

even to each other.

KEMPTON: Until when?

DI HOMES: By my reckoning, end of oh, 2012.

KEMPTON: What?

DI HOMES: Oh yes, it's not just Roy Jenkins, but Harold Wilson himself has decided it'll be the 21st century before this all comes out.

KEMPTON: What about the campaign?

DOTTY: Just sign it. Sign it.

KEMPTON signs the document.

DI HOMES: That's it - game over Kempton.

DI HOMES picks it up, folds it, and flourishes it in the air.

DI HOMES: This is going to outlast you - and me as well. I don't know about you, but I'm going to retire happy.

DI HOMES leaves.

KEMPTON: Forty years. You wouldn't have got that for murder.

JOHN: Can they stop your campaign like that? I'm sorry....

KEMPTON: I won't have made a difference. That's it. It's over. Probably best if you go now.

JOHN: Can I come back?

KEMPTON: No. Just go - while we put it all out of our heads again.

DOTTY: Don't Kempton...

JOHN: I'm sorry. It was just - stupid, stupid.

He exits.

DOTTY: So, you did it all for him. *(She smiles, sighs)* Cup of tea?

Music: Conversations / Cilla Black

Film (old cine footage of Kempton outside the Old Bailey)

Music: Misunderstood /The Monkeys

The end

Footnote

As a result of the case, the common law offence of larceny was abolished on 1 January 1969, for all purposes not relating to offences committed before that date. A clause was inserted into the Theft Act 1968, making it illegal to 'remove without authority any object displayed or kept for display to the public in a building to which the public has access'.

Kempton Bunton died in 1976. His and John's secret was only revealed when The National Archives released their signed statements in January 2012.

The Labour government introduced free TV licences for people aged over-75 from November 2000, a concession received by around 4.5 million households.

The BBC is primarily funded by licence fees. The level of the fee is set by Secretary of State for Digital, Culture, Media and Sport after consultation with the BBC. A key element of the licence fee settlement, announced in July 2015, was that the BBC would take over funding free licences for the over-75s.

From 1 August 2020, free licences have only been available to people aged over-75 who are in receipt of Pension Credit.